Education

London: H M S O

Researched and written by Reference Services, Central Office of Information.

This publication is an expanded version of the chapter on education which appears in *Britain 1993: An Official Handbook.*

ISBN 0 11 701733 7

HMSO publications are available from:
HMSO Publications Centre
(Mail, fax and telephone orders only)
PO Box 276, London SW8 5DT
Telephone orders 071-873 9090
General enquiries 071-873 0011
(queuing system in operation for both numbers)
Fax orders 071-873 8200

HMSO Bookshops
49 High Holborn, London WC1V 6HB   071-873 0011
Fax 071-873 8200 (counter service only)
258 Broad Street, Birmingham B1 2HE   021-643 3740   Fax 021-643 6510
Southey House, 33 Wine Street, Bristol BS1 2BQ
0272 264306   Fax 0272 294515
9-21 Princess Street, Manchester M60 8AS   061-834 7201   Fax 061-833 0634
16 Arthur Street, Belfast BT1 4GD   0232 238451   Fax 0232 235401
71 Lothian Road, Edinburgh EH3 9AZ   031-228 4181   Fax 031-229 2734
HMSO's Accredited Agents
(see Yellow Pages)

and through good booksellers

Contents

Acknowledgments

This book has been compiled with the co-operation of several organisations, including other government departments and agencies. The editor would like to thank all those who have contributed their comments, and in particular the Department for Education, the Scottish Office, the Welsh Office, and the Northern Ireland Information Office.

Photograph Credits
Photographs on pages 1–3 of the illustration section: Department for Education.

Introduction

British[1] education aims to develop fully the abilities of individuals, both young and old, for their own benefit and that of society as a whole. Compulsory schooling takes place between the ages of 4 or 5 and 16. Some provision is made for children under school age, and many pupils remain at school beyond the minimum leaving age. Post-school education, mainly at universities and institutions of further and higher education, is organised flexibly to provide a wide range of opportunities for academic and vocational education and continuing study throughout life.

Further information on developments in education is contained in *Current Affairs: A Monthly Survey*, published by HMSO.

[1] 'Britain' is used informally in this book to mean the United Kingdom of Great Britain and Northern Ireland. 'Great Britain' comprises England, Scotland and Wales.

Major Reforms

During the last few years the education service has undergone the most far-reaching reforms since 1945. The aims of the Government's policies are to:

—raise standards at all levels of ability;

—increase parental choice of schools and improve the partnership between parents and schools;

—make further and higher education more widely accessible and more responsive to the needs of the economy; and

—achieve the best possible return from the resources invested in the education service.

Schools

In schools, the Government is seeking to:

—improve school management;

—secure a broader and more balanced curriculum for all pupils so that they can develop the qualities and skills required for adult life and work in a technological age;

—ensure that examinations support curriculum objectives;

—implement schemes for the local management of schools; and

—improve the quality of teaching through better teacher training and appraisal.

Further proposals on education reform in England and Wales were set out in a White Paper, published in July 1992. The main proposals are:

—the introduction of measures to make it easier for schools to become grant-maintained (see p. 12);

—the establishment of a funding agency for grant-maintained schools;

—more specialisation by schools in their particular subject strengths;

—measures to improve bad schools;

—the setting up of a new body to improve standards in schools (see p. 31);

—the creation of a new, independent tribunal to hear parents' appeals against local education authority (LEA) decisions regarding their children who have special educational needs; and

—new powers to deal with the problem of surplus school places.

Fuller details are given in the relevant sections.

Schools are also encouraged to be more responsive to the needs of a multi-ethnic society. Measures are being taken to widen the choice of schools available and to ensure that schools respond effectively to the demands of parents and the broader community. The Government supports LEAs in their statutory responsibility to ensure that school governors are adequately trained.

Post-school Education

The Government's principal aims for further education and training (see p. 42) are to:

—ensure that participation becomes the norm for all 16- and 17-year-olds who can benefit from it;

—improve vocational qualifications in order to increase the proportion of young people and adults acquiring higher levels of skills and expertise; and

—secure the most efficient and effective use of resources.

The Government's main objectives for higher education (see p. 37) are to:

—secure enough places for suitably qualified and motivated students;

—ensure that the system maintains a high quality and becomes increasingly relevant to students' needs and to those of the economy and society as a whole; and

—ensure that suitable arrangements are made for student support.

In order to spread the benefits of higher education more widely, the Government encourages educational institutions to recruit more students from ethnic minority and other under-represented groups.

Legislation making major reforms in the funding and organisation of further and higher education has been passed by Parliament (see p. 35).

Administration and Finance

The Secretary of State for Education has overall responsibility for education in England, and for the Government's relations with and support for higher education colleges in England as well as universities throughout Great Britain. The Secretaries of State for Wales and for Scotland are responsible for non-university education in their countries, and are consulted about education in universities. The Secretary of State for Northern Ireland is responsible for both university and non-university education in the Province. From April 1993 each Secretary of State will be responsible for all higher education in his country.

The government departments responsible for education are the Department for Education in England, the Welsh Office Education Department, the Scottish Office Education Department, and the Department of Education for Northern Ireland. They formulate education policies and allocate some government funds to the local government authorities responsible for providing schools and other facilities. The departments are also responsible for the supply and training of teachers.

Most publicly financed school education, and that provided by local further education colleges, is the responsibility of local government education authorities. In England increasing numbers of schools are choosing to become grant-maintained (see p. 12). In Northern Ireland the education service is administered locally by five education and library boards.

LEAs employ teachers and other staff, provide and maintain buildings, supply equipment and materials and, in England and

Wales, award grants to students progressing to further and higher education.

From April 1993 further education colleges will be removed from local authority control and will receive public funding through separate further education funding councils in England and Wales, and direct from the Scottish Office Education Department in Scotland.

Estimated spending on education in Britain in 1991–92 was £29,300 million. About 70 per cent was incurred by LEAs, which make their own expenditure decisions according to local needs. Parts of the education service are funded by central government. The largest item of Department for Education spending is devoted to higher education. The Departments of Employment and of Trade and Industry also fund educational programmes; the former, for example, finances the Technical and Vocational Education Initiative (see p. 27) and Compacts (see p. 51).

Part of the Government's general revenue support—made by the Department of the Environment to local government authorities in England and by the Welsh Office in Wales—is allocated by the authorities to their education service. The Government also assists authorities' expenditure on educational activities of national priority. In 1992–93, for instance, the Government is contributing some £228 million towards a total of £377 million to be spent on projects, including the National Curriculum, local management of schools and colleges, teacher recruitment, support for information technology in schools and health education in schools. The rest of education authorities' expenditure is met by local taxation and non-domestic rates. In Scotland education is financed on a similar basis.

In Northern Ireland the costs of the education and library boards are met in full by the Department of Education.

The Government funds directly the current and capital costs of grant-maintained schools which have opted to leave local education authority control (see p. 12) and of city technology colleges (see p. 16) in England and Wales and comparable institutions in Scotland and Northern Ireland.

Higher Education

Higher education is largely financed by grants to individual institutions and tuition fees paid for students through the awards system. The Government has shifted the balance of public funding for full-time undergraduate higher education from the institutional grant to tuition fees paid for students. This is intended to create a more direct link between an institution's income and the number of its students and to encourage institutions to increase their efficiency by making full use of capacity.

Grants for universities in Great Britain are currently distributed by the Universities Funding Council (UFC), a statutory body. Certain individual establishments, such as the Open University, are financed directly by the Department for Education. In Northern Ireland grant is paid directly to the universities by the Department of Education, following advice from the UFC. The private University of Buckingham receives no public grant.

The Polytechnics and Colleges Funding Council is currently responsible for allocating public funds for higher courses in most colleges of higher education in England. Similar institutions in Wales are financed by the Welsh Office. Higher courses in Wales continue to be financed by local authorities. In Scotland all courses offered by the central institutions and colleges of education are funded by central government; advanced courses provided by local authority further education colleges are financed by the local authorities.

Universities and other higher education institutions undertake training, research or consultancy for commercial firms. The Government is encouraging them to secure a larger flow of funds from these sources. Many educational establishments have endowments or receive grants from foundations and benefactors.

Under legislation passed by Parliament in 1992, these financing arrangements will be changed. In England, Scotland and Wales, there will be separate funding councils responsible for allocating public funds on a fair basis to all higher education institutions, including the Open University. The Universities Funding Council and the Polytechnics and Colleges Funding Council will, therefore, be abolished in 1993 and replaced by the three new councils.

The Government reimburses in full the amount spent by local authorities on mandatory student maintenance grants and fees (see p. 37).

Schools

Parents are required by law to see that their children receive efficient full-time education, at school or elsewhere, between the ages of 5 and 16 in Great Britain and 4 and 16 in Northern Ireland. Some 9 million children attend Britain's 34,800 state and independent schools.

About 93 per cent of pupils receive free education financed from public funds, while the others attend independent schools financed from fees paid by parents.

Boys and girls are taught together in most primary schools. More than 80 per cent of pupils in maintained secondary schools in England and Wales and over 60 per cent in Northern Ireland attend mixed schools. In Scotland nearly all secondary schools are mixed. Most independent schools for younger children are co-educational; the majority providing secondary education are single-sex, although the number of mixed schools is growing.

Rights of Parents

Parents have a statutory right to express a preference for a particular school for their children, and have an effective channel of appeal at local level. Schools are obliged to publish their admissions criteria and basic information about themselves and their public examination results. In order to increase parental choice, primary and secondary schools are required to admit pupils up to the limit of their physical capacity if there is sufficient demand on behalf of children eligible for admission.

Legislation passed by Parliament in 1992 is designed to enable parents in England and Wales to make more informed choices about their children's education.

From the autumn of 1992 parents choosing among local secondary schools will:

— find freely available comparative tables showing the latest public examination results school by school; and

— find in each school's prospectus improved information on public examination results and truancy rates.

From 1993 regulations in England and Wales will require by law the inclusion in comparative tables of all local secondary schools, including independent ones; the tables will also include information on truancy rates, National Curriculum assessment results and the destinations of school leavers.

The legislation also provides for information to be given to parents on the findings of school inspection reports (see p. 31).

Regulations in England and Wales require all maintained schools to send to parents a written annual report on their child's progress. The report must contain:

— a commentary on the child's progress in subjects studied;

— details of the results of National Curriculum assessments and of public examinations taken by the child;

— comparative information about the results of other pupils of the same age in the school;

— details of the child's attendance record showing the number of unauthorised absences; and

— information about the arrangements for discussing the report with teachers at the school.

Management

England and Wales

Schools supported from public funds are of three main kinds:

—county schools are owned and maintained by local education authorities wholly out of public funds;

—voluntary aided and voluntary controlled schools, mostly established by religious denominations, are also wholly maintained from public funds but the governors of voluntary aided schools contribute to capital costs; and

—grant-maintained schools, which have chosen to opt out of local education authority control after an affirmative ballot by parents under the provisions of legislation passed in 1988.

Each publicly maintained school has a governing body which includes a balance of parent and teacher representatives and governors appointed by the LEA. Governing bodies work with the head of the school to determine its aims and curriculum policy, allocate the school budget, interview and appoint staff and foster good relations with parents and the local community.

The role of governing bodies has been further enlarged since 1990. LEAs will be delegating responsibility for the management of school budgets to all secondary schools and primary schools by April 1994. In April 1991, 38 per cent of schools in England had delegated budgets and this rose to over 70 per cent in April 1992. Under the system of delegation, the LEA allocates funds—largely on the basis of pupil numbers—to the school, which then takes responsibility for spending decisions. LEAs will also be required from April 1994 to extend local management to special schools; authorities will be required to fund special schools according to a formula and some schools will have delegated management powers.

Grant-maintained Schools

Grant-maintained schools are self-governing and are financed by central government. The governing body is made up of five elected parent governors, one or two teachers elected by the teachers at the school, the head teacher and eight or nine other governors. On a simple projection of current trends, there could be over 1,500 grant-maintained schools by April 1994. The Government hopes that in time all state schools will become grant-maintained. In the July 1992 White Paper the Government is proposing that a new statutory body, the Funding Agency for Schools, should be set up to calculate and pay grant to grant-maintained schools and be responsible for financial monitoring. The Agency will act under regulations and guidelines set down by the Secretary of State.

The Government is also proposing that small primary schools in rural areas should take advantage of the grant-maintained option. Under this, a cluster of small schools could become grant-maintained and be managed by a single governing body which would distribute funds to the individual schools. Each school would ballot parents on grant-maintained status.

LEAs will continue to be responsible for maintained schools which do not become grant-maintained.

Under the Government's proposals the Funding Agency would be responsible for securing sufficient school places when at least 75 per cent of secondary or primary pupils are educated in grant-maintained schools in a local authority area. This function would be shared between the Agency and the authority where more than 10 per cent of the pupils were educated in grant-maintained schools.

Scotland

In Scotland most of the schools supported from public funds are provided by education authorities and are known as public schools. Education authorities are required to establish school boards to play a significant part in the administration and management of schools. The boards consist of elected parent and staff members as well as co-opted members, thereby encouraging greater parental involvement and closer links between home, school and local community. Parents of children at public schools can opt for local self-management following approval by a ballot; such schools receive funding directly from central government instead of the local education authority.

Northern Ireland

The main categories of school supported by public funds are as follows:

— controlled schools provided by the education and library boards and managed through boards of governors;

— maintained schools managed by boards of governors with overall general management from the Council for Catholic Maintained Schools;

— voluntary grammar schools, which may be under Roman Catholic management or non-denominational boards of governors; and

— grant-maintained integrated schools taking Protestant and Roman Catholic pupils.

All grant-aided schools include elected parents and teachers on their boards of governors.

Although all schools must be open to pupils of all religions, most Roman Catholic pupils attend Catholic maintained schools or Catholic voluntary grammar schools and most Protestant children are enrolled at controlled schools or non-denominational voluntary grammar schools.

The Council for Catholic Maintained Schools has responsibility for all maintained schools under Roman Catholic management which are under the auspices of the diocesan authorities and of religious orders. The Council's main objective is to promote high standards of education in the schools for which it is responsible. Its membership consists of trustee representatives appointed by the Northern Irish bishops, of people appointed by the Department of Education in consultation with the bishops and of parents and teachers.

The Government has a statutory duty, set out in 1989 legislation, to encourage integrated education as a way of breaking down sectarian barriers. There are 16 integrated schools with 2,800 pupils.

New integrated schools receive immediate government funding. Existing controlled, maintained and voluntary grammar schools can also apply to become integrated following a majority vote by parents. There are two categories of integrated schools. Grant-maintained integrated status can be applied for by new and independent schools as well as those already receiving public funds. If this is approved, the school is funded directly by the Department of Education and run by a board of governors. Controlled integrated status can be sought by voluntary and controlled schools; education and library boards can also apply to set up such schools. The boards provide funding for, and supervise, controlled integrated schools.

Secondary school governors have delegated responsibility for managing school budgets and staff numbers. Primary and nursery school governors have delegated responsibility for managing non-staff costs only, although from April 1992 full delegation is being extended gradually into primary schools.

Nursery and Primary Schools

Although there is no statutory requirement to educate under-fives, successive governments have enabled nursery education to expand. Half of three- and four-year-olds receive education in nursery schools or classes or in infants' classes in primary schools. In addition, many children attend pre-school playgroups, most of which are organised by parents and incorporated in the Pre-School Playgroups Association.

Compulsory education begins at five in Great Britain and four in Northern Ireland, when children go to infant schools or departments; at seven many go on to junior schools or departments. The usual age for transfer from primary to secondary schools is 11 in England, Wales and Northern Ireland, but some local authorities in England have established first schools for pupils aged 5 to 8, 9 or 10 and middle schools for age-ranges between 8 and 14. In Scotland primary schools take children from 5 to 12.

Secondary Schools

Around nine-tenths of the maintained secondary school population in Great Britain attend comprehensive schools. These take pupils without reference to ability or aptitude and provide a wide range of secondary education for all or most of the children in a district. English and Welsh schools can be organised in a number of ways. They include:

—those that take the full secondary school age-range from 11 to 18;

—middle schools, whose pupils move on to senior comprehensive schools at 12, 13 or 14, leaving at 16 or 18; and

—schools with an age-range of 11 or 12 to 16, combined with a sixth-form or a tertiary college for pupils over 16.

Sixth-form colleges are schools which may provide non-academic in addition to academic courses. Tertiary colleges offer a range of full-time and part-time vocational courses for students over 16, as well as academic courses. From April 1993, sixth-form and tertiary colleges will be transferred to a new independent further education sector and be funded direct by national further education funding councils.

Most other children attend grammar or secondary modern schools, to which they are allocated after selection procedures at the age of 11.

Over 300 secondary schools have left local authority control and become grant-maintained (see p. 12).

There are 14 city technology colleges in England. While required to deliver the full range of the National Curriculum, the colleges place special emphasis on technology, science and business understanding. They are independent of LEAs and are established in partnership between central government and private and voluntary sponsors. They are introducing innovative curricular and management practices.

Building on the work of the colleges, a network of maintained secondary schools specialising in technology is being established. Some of these will operate as technology colleges, with sponsors playing a direct role in management through representation on the governing body.

The Government is also encouraging maintained schools wishing to specialise in subjects like science, music or modern languages, while still teaching the full National Curriculum.

The aim of Government policies is to increase the diversity of secondary schools and thereby increase parental choice.

Scottish secondary education is almost completely non-selective; the majority of schools are six-year comprehensives. The Government, in partnership with private sponsors, is seeking to set up technology academies in Scotland with a role similar to that of the city technology colleges.

In Northern Ireland secondary education is organised largely along selective lines, based on a system of testing. However, there are some secondary schools run on a non-selective basis.

Failing Schools

The Government has announced proposals designed to deal with poor schools in England and Wales. If school inspectors identified a school that was failing to give its pupils an acceptable standard of education, the local education authority would be able to appoint new governors and withdraw delegated management from the school. If these measures failed to work, the Secretary of State would be able to bring in an Education Association to put the school under new management until its performance had reached a satisfactory level. The new management would be financed from central government. After further advice from the Schools Inspectorate, the Secretary of State would decide whether to end the Association's period of care for the school. The school would be considered for grant-maintained status.

Independent Schools

Fee-paying independent schools must register with the appropriate education department and are open to inspection. They can be required to remedy serious shortcomings in their accommodation or instruction, and to exclude anyone regarded as unsuitable to teach in or own a school. About 7 per cent of school children attend independent schools.

There are 2,475 independent schools educating 608,000 pupils of all ages. They charge fees varying from around £300 a term for day pupils at nursery age to £3,500 a term for senior boarding pupils. Many offer bursaries to help pupils from less wealthy families. Such pupils may also be helped by LEAs—particularly if the authorities' own schools cannot meet the needs of individual children—or by the Government's Assisted Places Scheme, under which assistance is given according to parental income. Over 37,000 places are offered in England, Wales and Scotland under the scheme. The Government also gives income-related help with fees to pupils at certain specialist music and ballet schools.

Independent schools range from small kindergartens to large day and boarding schools and from new and in some cases experimental schools to ancient foundations. The 600 boys', girls' and mixed preparatory schools prepare children for entry to senior schools. The normal age-range for these preparatory schools is from 7 to 11, 12 or 13, but many of the schools now have pre-preparatory departments for younger children. A number of independent schools have been established by religious and ethnic minorities.

Independent schools for older pupils—from 11, 12 or 13 to 18 or 19—include about 550 which are often referred to as public schools, and which belong to the Headmasters' Conference, the

Governing Bodies Association, the Society of Headmasters and Headmistresses of Independent Schools, the Girls' Schools Association and the Governing Bodies of Girls' Schools Association. They should not be confused with the state-supported public schools in Scotland.

Special Educational Needs

Special educational needs comprise learning difficulties of all kinds, including mental and physical disabilities which hinder or prevent learning. In the case of children whose learning difficulties are severe or complex, LEAs are required to:

—identify, assess and secure provision for their needs; and

—give parents the right to be involved in decisions about their child's special education.

If the education authority believes that it should determine the special education provision for the child, it must draw up a formal statement of the child's special educational needs and the action it intends to take to meet them. Parents have a right of appeal if they disagree with the special educational provision set out in the statement.

Wherever possible, children with special educational needs are educated in ordinary schools, provided that the parents' wishes have been taken into account, and that this is compatible with meeting the needs of the child, with the provision of efficient education for the other children in the school, and with the efficient use of resources.

Because of concern about the way these arrangements are working the Government is proposing to:

—set statutory time limits within which the education authority must carry out procedures for making assessments and statements;

—require the education authority to comply with parents' choice of school unless this would be inappropriate for the child or involve an inefficient use of resources; and

—establish an independent tribunal to hear appeals against education authority decisions. The tribunal's decisions would be binding on all parties to the case and it would replace the present system of appeals to local committees and to the Secretary of State.

The Government is also proposing to change the law to ensure that an LEA or grant-maintained school named in a statement of special educational needs should be required to admit the child. The education authority would have to consult the governors before naming the school. In future, it is intended that parents will be given the right to ballot on grant-maintained status for special schools.

In Scotland the choice of school is a matter for agreement between education authorities and parents.

There are 1,900 special schools (both day and boarding), including those run by voluntary organisations and those established in hospitals. They cater for about 125,000 pupils with special educational needs who cannot be educated at ordinary schools. Developments in information technology (see p. 31) are increasingly leading to better quality education for these children.

Teachers

Teachers in publicly maintained schools are appointed by LEAs or school governing bodies. Over 500,000 teachers are employed in maintained and independent schools, and the average pupil-teacher ratio for all schools is about 17 to 1. Teachers in maintained schools must hold qualifications approved by the appropriate education department (see p. 46).

Formal teacher appraisal is being introduced in English and Welsh schools. By 1995 all teachers will have completed the first year of their appraisal cycles.

Health and Welfare of Schoolchildren

Physical education, including organised games, is part of the curriculum of all maintained schools, and playing fields must be available for pupils over the age of eight. Most secondary schools have a gymnasium.

Government health departments are responsible for the medical inspection of schoolchildren and for advice on, and treatment of, medical and dental problems associated with children of school age. The Government believes that the education service has a role to play in preventing and dealing with juvenile drug misuse and in helping to prevent the spread of AIDS. Government funds have supported the appointment in most LEAs of drugs and health education co-ordinators for schools, colleges and the youth service.

Local education authorities are largely free to decide what milk, meals or other refreshment to offer at their schools, and the charges to make. Provision has to be made free of charge, however, for pupils from families receiving certain social security benefits. Under certain conditions the authorities must supply free school transport, and they have discretionary powers to help with the cost of travel to school. In Northern Ireland school meals must be provided for primary, special and grant-aided nursery school pupils.

Corporal punishment is prohibited by law in maintained schools in Britain.

The Curriculum and Examinations

England and Wales

The Government favours widening educational opportunities as much as possible through a broad and balanced curriculum designed to meet the individual needs of pupils and relevant to the modern world.

In 1989 primary and secondary schools in England and Wales began the gradual introduction of the National Curriculum. This consists of the core subjects of English, mathematics, science, and religious education (see p. 24), as well as the other foundation subjects of history, geography, technology, music, art, physical education and, for secondary level pupils, a modern foreign language.

The National Curriculum subjects are being introduced progressively by year group, and from September 1992 all subjects had been taught to at least one year group in both primary and secondary schools. The core subjects will be taught to all pupils from the age of 5 to 16 in the academic year 1995–96 and the entire National Curriculum will be taught to all pupils in this age group from the academic year 1996–97.

In Wales the Welsh language constitutes a core subject in Welsh-speaking schools and a foundation subject elsewhere under the National Curriculum. Some 80 per cent of primary schools use Welsh either as a teaching medium or teach it as a second language, while nearly 90 per cent of secondary schools teach Welsh as a first or second language.

The National Curriculum requirements for each subject are laid down in statutory orders comprising attainment targets and statements of attainment specifying the knowledge, skills and understanding expected of pupils at different levels. Programmes of study set out what should be taught in the key stages of schooling. Arrangements for testing pupils against the attainment targets at the ages of 7, 11, 14 and 16 are laid down in statutory assessment orders. The first national statutory assessment of 7-year-olds was undertaken in 1991. The first for 11-year-olds will take place in 1994, and that for 14-year-olds in 1993. Pupils' performance in relation to attainment targets is assessed and reported on at the four key stages. Regulations have been introduced covering the manner and form in which assessments of individual pupils are to be made available to parents and others (see p. 10).

Scotland

The content and management of the curriculum are the responsibility of education authorities and head teachers, though guidance is provided by the Secretary of State for Scotland and the Scottish Consultative Council on the Curriculum. The Council has recommended that secondary level pupils should follow a broad and balanced curriculum consisting of English, mathematics, science, a modern European language, social studies, technological activities, art, music or drama, religious and moral education, and physical education. A major programme of curricular review and development is in progress for the 5-to-14 age-range. The Government is in the process of issuing new guidelines on all aspects of the curriculum and assessment. Standardised tests in English and mathematics are being introduced for primary school pupils at stages 4 and 7, normally at ages 8 and 12. The Government wants to promote the teaching of foreign languages in primary schools and pilot studies are in progress. It also intends that all pupils should study a foreign language during their compulsory secondary education.

A committee has been established to review courses and assessment arrangements in the final two years of secondary schooling. Provision is made for teaching in Gaelic in Gaelic-speaking areas.

Northern Ireland

A common curriculum is being introduced in all Northern Ireland grant-aided schools. It is based on six broad areas of study: English, mathematics, science and technology, the environment and society, creative and expressive studies and, for secondary schools, language studies. The curriculum will be fully implemented by September 1993.

Attainment targets, programmes of study and methods of assessment—at ages 8, 11, 14 and 16—are specified for all compulsory subjects. The first assessments at the ages of 11 and 14 will take place in 1994 and at the age of 8 and 16 in 1995. In addition, the school curriculum includes six compulsory cross-curricular themes: education for mutual understanding, cultural heritage, health education, information technology and, in secondary schools, economic awareness and careers education. Pupils are learning from a common history curriculum in the environment and society area of study.

Religious Education and Collective Worship in Schools

In England and Wales maintained schools must provide religious education and a daily act of collective worship. In county schools, and in some kinds of voluntary schools, religious education must be taught according to a locally agreed syllabus. Under legislation passed in 1988, new agreed syllabuses have been required to take account of the fact that the religious traditions in Britain are in the main Christian; the teaching of the other main religions represented in Britain are also covered. Since the 1988 legislation, many LEAs have reviewed their agreed syllabuses; the Government is proposing that those who have not yet done so should be required to do so in a specified period. Each local education authority area has a standing council which advises the authority on the development of religious education.

In all voluntary schools there is the opportunity for denominational religious education. Collective worship is within the control of the governing body.

Parents have the right to withdraw their children from religious education classes and from collective worship.

Scottish education authorities are required to see that schools practise religious observance and give pupils religious instruction; parents may withdraw their children if they wish. Certain schools provide for Roman Catholic children but in all schools there are safeguards for the individual conscience.

In Northern Ireland, too, schools are obliged to offer religious education and collective worship, although parents have the right to withdraw their children from both. In controlled schools clergy have a right of access which may be used for denominational instruction. In voluntary schools collective worship and religious education are controlled by the management authorities. It is intended that religious education will have an agreed core syllabus which grant-aided schools can expand according to their own needs and wishes.

Ethnic Minority Children

Most school-aged children from ethnic minorities were born in Britain and tend to share the interests and aspirations of children in the population at large. Nevertheless, a substantial number still have particular needs arising from cultural differences, including those of language, religion and custom.

The education authorities have done much to meet these needs. English language teaching continues to receive priority, with a growing awareness of the value of bilingual support in the early primary years to facilitate the learning of English. Schools may teach the main ethnic minority community languages at secondary level as part of the National Curriculum. Emphasis has been placed on the need for schools to take account of the ethnic and cultural backgrounds of pupils. Measures have been taken to improve the achievement of ethnic minority pupils, and to prepare all children, not just those of ethnic minority origin, for living in a multi-ethnic society.

Curriculum Development

In England curriculum development is promoted by the National Curriculum Council and in Wales by the Curriculum Council for Wales. Both bodies keep the curriculum for maintained schools under review, advise the Government on content, carry out programmes of research and development and publish information relating to the curriculum. The Government proposes to set up a new Authority in England to ensure quality in the curriculum and the associated assessment arrangements. This will replace the National Curriculum Council and the School Examinations and Assessment Council (see p. 29). Similar action is being taken in Wales.

In Scotland curriculum development is undertaken by the Scottish Consultative Council on the Curriculum and in Northern Ireland by the Northern Ireland Curriculum Council.

Technical and Vocational Education Initiative

The Technical and Vocational Education Initiative (TVEI) applies in England, Scotland and Wales. It is financed and administered by the Department of Employment, the Scottish Office Industry Department and the Welsh Office, working in close co-operation with local education authorities. It is intended that the education of 14- to 18-year-olds should equip them for working life by ensuring that the school curriculum relates to the working environment, and by improving skills and qualifications, particularly in science, technology and modern languages. Over a million students are benefiting from TVEI in England.

Examinations and Qualifications

England, Wales and Northern Ireland

The General Certificate of Secondary Education (GSCE) is the main examination taken by secondary school pupils in England, Wales and Northern Ireland around the age of 16. GCSE examinations are usually taken after five years of secondary education and can lead on to more advanced education and training. The GCSE will be the main means of assessing pupils' progress in the last two years of compulsory education. Assessment for the core subjects of the National Curriculum started in September 1992 for first examination in 1994 and the remaining foundation subjects will be progressively assessed over subsequent years. The structure of the GCSE examination is being adapted to accord with National Curriculum requirements.

The General Certificate of Education (GCE) Advanced (A) level is normally taken after a further two years of study. New examinations—Advanced Supplementary (AS) levels—were held for the first time in 1989 and enable sixth-form pupils to study a wider range of subjects than was possible before. Students specialising in the arts and humanities, for example, can continue to study mathematics and technological subjects at the new level. Requiring the same standard of work but with only half the content of A levels, an AS level occupies half the teaching and study time of an A level. A levels or a mixture of A and AS levels are the main standard for entrance to higher education and to many forms of professional training.

Discussions have taken place with the main vocational examining and validating bodies regarding their possible contribution to courses and qualifications for 14- to 16-year-olds. It is expected that courses will be available from September 1993 which will extend the study of National Curriculum subjects, particularly technology, into vocational and practical areas for those pupils whose aptitudes lie in this direction.

The Certificate of Pre-Vocational Education is for those at school or college wishing to continue in full-time education for a year after the age of 16 and to receive a broadly-based preparation for work or vocational and other courses. The Certificate is being developed by the City and Guilds of London Institute. An improved version will be called the City and Guilds Diploma of Vocational Education. Business & Technology Education Council (BTEC) qualifications can also serve as a preparation for work or a stepping-stone into higher education. Schools are now allowed to offer BTEC First Diploma courses to 16- to 19-year-olds.

Scotland

Scottish pupils take the Scottish Certificate of Education (SCE) at Standard grade at the end of their fourth year of secondary education (equivalent to the fifth year in England and Wales). Pupils in the fifth and sixth years sit the SCE Higher grade; passes at this grade are the basis for entry to higher education or professional training. However, entry is becoming more flexible as wider access to under-represented groups with non-standard qualifications is encouraged. The Certificate of Sixth Year Studies (CSYS) is for pupils who have completed their Higher grade main studies and who wish to continue studies in particular subjects. Standard grade courses and examinations cater for the whole ability range. Higher and CSYS examinations are being revised to ensure compatibility with the Standard grade.

The National Certificate is for students over 16 who have successfully completed a programme of vocational courses based on short study units.

Examinations and Assessment Councils

All GCSE and other qualifications offered to pupils of compulsory school age in maintained schools in England and Wales must be approved by the Government. Associated syllabuses and assessment procedures must comply with national guidelines and be approved by the School Examinations and Assessment Council. The aim is to secure a reasonably wide choice of qualifications and syllabuses which promote a broad and balanced curriculum and support the National Curriculum.

The Council keeps under review all aspects of examinations and assessment in England and Wales. It liaises with the National Curriculum Council for England and the Curriculum Council for

Wales on work connected with the National Curriculum in schools. The Government is proposing to replace the Council with another body (see p. 26).

The Council's Evaluation and Monitoring Unit evaluates the assessment arrangements for the National Curriculum.

The equivalent body in Scotland is the Scottish Examination Board, which liaises with the Scottish Consultative Council on the Curriculum. The Scottish Assessment of Achievement research programme has surveyed attainments of pupils in English and mathematics at the ages of 8, 12 and 14.

The Northern Ireland Schools Examinations and Assessment Council is responsible for keeping all aspects of examinations and assessment under review. It liaises with the Northern Ireland Curriculum Council.

Progress Reports

Parents in England and Wales receive a yearly progress report on their child's National Curriculum achievements, general progress and results in public examinations (see p. 10). The National Record of Achievement, launched in February 1991, is designed to present a simple record of achievement in education and training throughout working life.

In Scotland the report card system is being reformed to give parents a clearer view of their children's progress. In Northern Ireland all pupils will be issued with a record of achievement on leaving primary and secondary education.

Educational Standards

Her Majesty's Inspectorate (HMI) has traditionally reported to the Government on the quality of education in schools and most further and higher education establishments outside the universities, and advised education authorities and schools as well as the Government. It has also reported on the youth service and education provision in hospitals, prisons and youth custody centres, and the armed services. LEAs employ inspectors or advisers to guide them on maintained schools.

In September 1992 new Offices independent of government were established in England and Wales, headed by Her Majesty's Chief Inspector of Schools in England and Her Majesty's Chief Inspector of Schools in Wales. The English Office is known as the Office for Standards in Education. In addition to advising the Government on quality, standards and efficiency in school education, the Chief Inspectors and their staff are responsible for regulating a new system of school inspections. Every school will have to be inspected regularly by independent inspectors to agreed national standards which will be monitored by the Offices. It is planned to examine 6,000 schools a year in England over a four-year period and this work will continue in four-yearly cycles. Parents will be sent a readable summary of the full inspection report, which will be published. Governors will have to prepare action plans to follow it up and then report back to parents on their progress. The new schools inspection system starts in 1993 for secondary schools and 1994 for primary and other schools.

In Northern Ireland school inspections are carried out by the Education and Training Inspectorate, which is part of the Department of Education.

Information Technology

The National Curriculum places a strong emphasis on the use of information technology (IT). In 1987 the Government announced a major new strategy to encourage use of educational technology across the curriculum so that pupils become familiar with the new technologies and use them to enhance learning. Between 1988 and 1992 the average number of microcomputers in English primary schools rose from 2.5 to 7, and in English secondary schools from 23 to 60; over two-thirds of teachers have undertaken awareness training in the use of IT. In Wales, the average number of pupils per microcomputer in primary schools went down from 68 to 34 between 1988 and 1991; in secondary schools over the same period the average number decreased from 30 to 14.

From 1991 to 1994 grants continue to increase the numbers of microcomputers in schools and for teacher training. They may be used to provide IT support for children with communication difficulties. In 1992–93 and 1993–94 grants are available to help secondary schools to buy CD-ROM (compact disc read only memory) drives and discs.

In each of the three years 1991–92 to 1993–94 there are grant-supported spending programmes of around £30 million to provide continuing support for IT in schools.

The Government is also making a grant of about £5 million a year to support the National Council for Educational Technology (NCET). The NCET was set up by the Government in 1988 to support, encourage, develop and apply the use of learning systems and new technologies, including microcomputers, electronic systems and other aspects of IT, to education and training. The corresponding body in Scotland is the Scottish Council for Educational Technology.

Other recent and current government funding includes:

—£750,000 for the development of 19 new National Curriculum software packages. The discs have been completed and are being used in a £400,000 pilot scheme to investigate the potential of interactive video as a teaching aid;

—£410,000 to install information relating to the National Curriculum on NERIS (National Educational Resources Information Service—an electronic database (see p. 34);

(see p. 34)

—£1.3 million for the development of five mathematics interactive video discs;

—£700,000 towards the cost of developing new CD-ROM titles in support of the National Curriculum;

—£40,000 towards the development of software to give blind and partially sighted students full access to CD-ROM materials; and

—£150,000 to help teacher training institutions to buy CD-ROM drives and discs.

In Wales the Welsh Office has financed the provision of satellite receiving equipment for secondary schools throughout the country.

In Northern Ireland, information technology is one of the six compulsory educational themes forming part of the curriculum for all pupils of statutory school age in grant-aided schools. The objectives of the IT theme are:

—knowledge, understanding and skills in IT;

—application of IT;

—enhancing the quality of learning, living and working through IT; and

—evaluating the impact of IT.

Educational Aids

Teachers and pupils use a range of aids to assist the processes of teaching and learning. The government-funded National Educational Resources Information Service enables schools to find out about teaching aids. Most schools have audio-visual equipment such as slide projectors and overhead projectors, and educational broadcasting is of major importance. The BBC and the independent broadcasting companies transmit radio and television programmes designed for schools. Teachers' notes, pupils' pamphlets and computer software accompany many broadcast series. All primary and secondary schools use microcomputers (see p. 32).

Careers Education and Guidance

Careers education is used to raise awareness of further and higher education and careers opportunities and helps young people to prepare for working life. The work of the Careers Service, run by LEAs, is supported by careers information material produced by the Government's Careers and Occupational Information Centre. A computer-assisted careers guidance system with substantial funding from the Government has been developed for students in higher education.

The Government has encouraged LEAs to enter into partnership with Training and Enterprise Councils and Local Enterprise Companies (see p. 52) to oversee the operation of the Careers Service locally. Under new proposals, the Government will be able to contract with a range of different organisations to provide a Careers Service which is more responsive to the needs of local people and employers.

In Northern Ireland, careers education is one of the six compulsory education themes forming part of the school curriculum.

Post-school Education

Legislation passed in 1992 is designed to transform post-compulsory education and training in England, Wales and Scotland. The reforms are ending the distinction between universities, polytechnics and other higher education establishments. New higher education funding councils in England, Scotland and Wales will be responsible for allocating public funds for teaching and general research. New links will be created to continue the present close relationship with Northern Ireland's existing unitary structure. Degree-awarding powers are being extended to all major higher education institutions and there will be new quality-assurance arrangements. Polytechnics have generally taken advantage of the right to call themselves universities.

Further-education and sixth-form colleges will become autonomous institutions outside LEA control, financed through new and separate further education funding councils for England and Wales from April 1993. By the mid-1990s, all 16- and 17-year-olds leaving full-time education in Great Britain will be encouraged to undertake vocational education or training by the offer of a training credit, enabling them to buy training from the establishment of their choice.

Every 16- and 17-year-old in Great Britain is guaranteed a place in full-time education or training.

Post-school education takes place at universities, the Scottish central institutions and colleges of education, further and higher education colleges, adult education centres, colleges of technology, colleges of art and design, and agricultural and horticultural colleges. There are also many independent specialist establishments, such as secretarial and correspondence colleges, and colleges for teaching English as a foreign language. Voluntary and public bodies offer cultural and general education, sometimes with assistance from LEAs and central government. Education and training schemes can be run by public or private organisations.

The Credit Accumulation and Transfer Scheme is used by many English and Welsh further and higher education establishments. In Scotland a credit accumulation scheme covers courses in all further and higher education. Opportunities for further and higher education and training are publicised by national information services, such as the Educational Counselling and Credit Transfer Information Service, which is largely funded by the Department for Education.

The Further Education Unit, with funding from the Department for Education and the Welsh Office, is an advisory and development body for further education. The Scottish Further Education Unit performs a parallel role.

Students

The proportion of young people entering higher education rose from 1 in 8 in 1980 to 1 in 5 by 1990 and is expected to reach 1 in 3 by the year 2000. One of the Government's main aims is to change the balance of provision in favour of scientific, technological and directly vocational courses.

Around 1.5 million students in Britain are taking full-time post-school education courses, including sandwich courses, where substantial periods of full-time study alternate with periods of supervised experience on a relevant job. There are also 4 million part-time enrolments, one half of whom are in adult education.

Morning assembly at a county first school.

Pupils working on a project to make a braille notewriter.

A sixth form computing resource centre.

A BTEC art and design course.

Working on
an Urdu
language
course.

A City and
Guilds general
catering course.

An economics course at
Worcester College of
Higher Education.

Studying for a
BSc in textiles.

Trinity College, Cambridge.

Leicester University's Centre of Education and Research.

Student Grants and Loans

Over 90 per cent of full-time students in England and Wales on first degree and other comparable higher education courses are eligible for mandatory awards. They cover tuition fees and maintenance, with parents contributing to maintenance costs according to income. They are awarded by local education authorities in England and Wales for courses leading up to first degree or comparable level of qualification. Grants for other courses are given at the discretion of an LEA. Similar schemes are administered by the Scottish Office Education Department and the Northern Ireland education and library boards. Grants for post-graduate study are offered by the Government education departments, the British Academy and the five research councils. Some scholarships are available from endowments and also from particular industries or companies.

Most students in full-time higher education up to first degree level can get a loan from the Student Loans Company each year to help meet their living costs. Loans are worth up to £830 in 1992–93 and are not means-tested. They are indexed to inflation. At present, most borrowers repay their loans over five years. They may put off their repayments for a year at a time if their income is below 85 per cent of average earnings. Student loans help share the cost of student support between students, parents and taxpayers in general.

Higher Education

Higher education is provided in the form of degree and other courses of a standard higher than the General Certificate of Education Advanced level or its equivalent. The Government considers that access to higher education courses should be available to all those who can benefit from them and have the necessary intellectual competence, motivation and maturity.

Although GCE A levels and their equivalents in Scotland have traditionally been the standard for entry to higher education courses, other qualifications and courses are now considered equally appropriate. These are AS levels, BTEC and other vocational qualifications (see p. 43) and access/foundation courses (see p. 40). The Scottish Wider Access Programme (SWAP) is designed to promote wider participation in higher education, especially by more mature students and those without the normal entry requirements. Successful completion of a SWAP course guarantees a higher education place.

In order to maintain British expertise in technology, recent government schemes have sought to expand higher education and research in electronics, engineering and computer science by making available extra student places, and additional staff and research fellowships. A Graduate Enterprise Programme offers 450 places on management training courses for recently qualified graduates.

Universities

There are 79 universities, including the Open University. They are governed by royal charters or by Act of Parliament and enjoy complete academic freedom. They appoint their own staff, decide which students to admit, provide their own courses and award their own degrees. The universities of Oxford and Cambridge date from the twelfth and thirteenth centuries, and the Scottish universities of St Andrews, Glasgow, Aberdeen and Edinburgh from the fourteenth and fifteenth centuries. All the other universities in Britain were founded in the nineteenth and twentieth centuries. The 1960s saw considerable expansion in the number of universities and students. The number of universities increased considerably in 1992, when polytechnics and some other higher education establishments were given the freedom to obtain university status and chose to exercise it.

Admission to universities is by selection. Of the 353,000 full-time home and overseas university students in 1990–91, excluding those at the University of Buckingham, 64,000 were postgraduate. There are just under 30,000 full-time university teachers paid wholly from university funds. The ratio of staff to full-time students is about 1 to 11. Except at the Open University, first degree courses are mainly full time and usually last three years. However, there are some four-year courses, and medical and veterinary courses normally require five years.

Degree titles vary according to the practice of each university. In England, Wales and Northern Ireland the most common titles for a first degree are Bachelor of Arts (BA) or Bachelor of Science (BSc) and for a second degree Master of Arts (MA), Master of Science (MSc), and Doctor of Philosophy (PhD). In the older Scottish universities Master is used for a first degree in arts subjects. Uniformity of standards between universities is promoted by employing external examiners for all university examinations.

Research is an important feature of university work; most staff combine research with their teaching duties and about half of postgraduate students are engaged on research projects. The Government has been seeking greater accountability and selectivity in research. It is encouraging universities to co–operate closely with industry on research projects.

Since 1967 a major contribution to post-school education in England and Wales has been made by polytechnics, most of which were established after 1967 and have now become universities, with the freedom to award their own degrees from 1993. They offer courses in a wide range of subjects, including those leading to first and higher degrees and graduate-equivalent qualifications. They also run courses leading to the examinations of the chief professional bodies, and to qualifications such as those of the Business & Technology Education Council.

Access and foundation courses provide a preparation and an appropriate test before enrolment on a course of higher education for prospective students who possess non-standard entry qualifications. Many are from the ethnic minority communities. The growth of access courses has been very rapid in recent years; about 600 are now available nationwide.

Polytechnics traditionally had close links with commerce and industry, and many students have jobs and attend on a part-time basis. Similar provision is made in Scotland in the 13 central institutions (which include polytechnics) and 50 further education colleges, and in Northern Ireland by the University of Ulster.

In England and Wales institutes and colleges of higher education, formed by the integration of teacher training with the rest of higher education, account for a significant proportion of higher education students. Some further education colleges run higher education courses, often of a specialised nature.

Large numbers of students on higher education courses in Great Britain in polytechnics and other higher education institutions have taken courses leading to the award of degrees and other academic qualifications by the Council for National Academic Awards (CNAA). The CNAA will be abolished in 1993, since higher education institutions will be free to award their own degrees. Those higher education institutions not awarding their own degrees will come to an arrangement with a local university, while others will approach the Open University, which will offer a national degree-awarding service.

A United Kingdom-wide Higher Education Quality Council is being established by the higher education institutions to monitor their quality control arrangements.

Admissions to universities are handled by the Universities Central Council for Admissions (UCCA). Admissions to other higher education institutions are arranged by the Polytechnics Central Admissions System (PCAS). Both bodies are to merge and are aiming to provide a single admissions system in time for applications leading to 1994 entry. Both organisations publish handbooks listing courses and giving guidance on admissions; these are available from schools, careers offices or from UCCA/PCAS, PO Box 67, Cheltenham, GL50 3SF. The qualifications needed to enter a course are determined by the institution concerned, as is the number of students admitted.

Open University
The Open University is a non-residential university offering degree and other courses for adult students of all ages in Britain and other parts of Europe. It uses a combination of specially produced printed texts, correspondence tuition, television and radio broadcasts, audio and video cassettes, and residential schools. There is also a network of study centres for contact with part-time tutors and counsellors, and with fellow students. No formal academic qualifications are required to register for most courses, but the standard of the University's degrees is the same as that of other universities. Its first degree is the BA (Open), a general degree awarded on a system of credits for each course completed.

The University has a programme of higher degrees, Bachelor of Philosophy (BPhil), MPhil and PhD, available through research; and MA, MSc and Master of Business Administration (MBA) through taught courses. About 7,500 students were registered on higher degree courses in 1992.

The University also has programmes for professionals in education and health and social welfare services, and for updating managers, scientists and technologists. Some of these are presented as multi-media courses taught in a similar way to courses in the undergraduate programme, and others are in the form of self-contained study packs.

The University has advised many other countries on setting up similar institutions. It has made a substantial contribution to the new Commonwealth of Learning project, which brings together distance-teaching establishments and students throughout the Commonwealth.

Further Education

Further education in England, Wales and Northern Ireland comprises all provision outside schools to people aged over 16, up to and including GCE A level or equivalent. Courses are run by over 500 colleges of further education, many of which also offer higher education courses.

Most of these colleges are currently controlled by LEAs but from April 1993 they will become autonomous institutions financed by further education funding councils. They will be controlled by further education corporations consisting of 10 to 20 members, including substantial representation from the business community.

In Scotland the new modular courses at the non-advanced level (see p. 29) can be taken in schools, further education colleges or as part of government training schemes.

Much further education is work-related and vocational, although most colleges also provide non-vocational courses, including GCSE and GCE A level courses. The system is flexible and enables the student to acquire whatever qualifications his or her capabilities and time allow.

Many students on further education courses attend part-time, either by day release or block release from employment or during the evenings. The further education system has strong ties with commerce and industry and co-operation with business is encouraged by the Government and its agencies. Employers are normally involved in designing courses.

Further education colleges supply much of the education element in training programmes like Youth Training and Employment Training, both sponsored by the Department of Employment. All young people on Youth Training are offered training and vocational education leading to qualifications at or equivalent to a minimum of level 2 in the framework established by the National Council for Vocational Qualifications and the Scottish Vocational Education Council.

Vocational Qualifications

The National Council for Vocational Qualifications (NCVQ) was set up in 1986 to reform and rationalise the vocational qualifications system in England, Wales and Northern Ireland. It is establishing a new framework of National Vocational Qualifications (NVQs) based on defined levels of achievement to which qualifications in all sectors can be assigned or accredited. The five levels are as follows:

Level 1 Competence in the performance of a range of work activities, most of which may be routine.

Level 2 Competence in a significant range of work activities, some of which are complex or non-routine, and require some responsibility.

Level 3 Competence in a broad range of work activities, most of which are complex and non-routine.

Level 4 Competence in a significant range of complex technical or professional work activities performed in a wide variety of contexts with a substantial degree of personal responsibility.

Level 5 Competence involving the application of a significant range of fundamental principles and complex techniques in a wide variety of contexts; very substantial personal autonomy and often significant responsibility for the work of others and for the allocation of substantial resources are strongly featured.

The first four levels have started operating and coverage will be virtually complete by the end of 1994. The Government is committed to the achievement of national education and training targets, one of which is that 50 per cent of the employed workforce should have attained NVQ level 3 or an equivalent qualification by the year 2000.

The Council is also working on the development of broadly based qualifications for inclusion within the NVQ framework, which will prepare young people for a range of related occupations and provide progression to higher education.

The competence-based system is being extended in Scotland through a new system of Scottish Vocational Qualifications

(SVQs). Along the lines of NVQs, SVQs are accredited by the Scottish Vocational Education Council. NVQs and SVQs have equal recognition throughout Britain.

Under recent legislation, more general job-related qualifications will be devised for those seeking a broad preparation for employment. The Government will promote equality of status for academic and vocational qualifications by developing new Ordinary and Advanced Diplomas. Students gaining an appropriate number of GSCE passes, equivalent vocational qualifications or a combination of these will receive the Ordinary Diploma. The Advanced Diploma will be awarded to those passing GCE A level and AS level examinations, students gaining vocational qualifications at the same level, and those with passes in a mixture of the two.

Other Examining Bodies

The Business & Technology Education Council (BTEC) plans and administers a unified national system of courses at all levels for students in industry, commerce and public administration in England, Wales and Northern Ireland.

The Scottish Vocational Education Council (SCOTVEC) is the principal examining and awarding body in the field of further education in Scotland. A flexible system of vocational courses for 16- to 18-year-olds, based on short units of study, has been introduced in schools and colleges in disciplines like business and administration, engineering and industrial production. These courses are also intended to meet the needs of many adults entering training or returning to education. The courses lead to the award of the non-advanced National Certificate. Similar courses are also available at advanced levels.

Qualifications in a range of occupational areas are offered by the City and Guilds of London Institute, and qualifications in commercial and office practice are awarded by the Royal Society of Arts.

Teacher Training

Almost all entrants to teaching in maintained and special schools in England and Wales complete a recognised course of initial teacher training. Such courses are offered by university departments of education as well as other higher education establishments. Non-graduates usually qualify by taking a four-year Bachelor of Education (BEd) honours degree. There are also specially designed two-year BEd courses—mostly in subjects where there is a shortage of teachers at the secondary level—for suitably qualified people. Graduates normally take a one-year Postgraduate Certificate of Education (PGCE) course. Two-year PGCE courses are available in the secondary shortage subjects for those whose first degree in an associated subject included at least one year's study of the subject they intend to teach.

Reforms

Under new government reforms in England and Wales, schools will play a much larger part in initial teacher training as full partners of higher education institutions. Under new criteria which will come into force in the period between September 1992 and September 1994, the amount of time spent by students in schools during teacher training is being increased so that at least two-thirds of training will take place in the classroom. Graduates on a 36-week, one-year course, for instance, will train in schools for at least 24 weeks instead of 15.

The Government expects that partner schools and institutions will exercise a joint responsibility for planning and managing courses and for the selection, training and assessment of students. Schools will train students to teach their specialist subjects, assess pupils and manage classes; they will also supervise students and assess their competence. Higher education institutions will be responsible for ensuring that courses meet requirements for academic validation, presenting courses for accreditation and awarding qualifications to successful students.

Accreditation

Institutions, rather than courses, will be accredited. An institution will have to submit a five-year development programme to the Council for the Accreditation of Teacher Education (CATE). An inspection by the Offices of Her Majesty's Inspector of Schools for England and for Wales will then take place, followed by a response from the institution. CATE will consider the inspectorate's report and the response and then make a recommendation to the Secretary of State, who will take the final decision on accreditation.

Other Training

Articled teacher courses, offering school-based training for graduates, were introduced in 1990. Trainees, who receive a bursary, take on a progressively greater teaching load, and formal training is provided both in initial teacher-training institutions and in school by college tutors and school teachers.

In 1989 the Government introduced a licensed teacher scheme in England and Wales for people without formal teacher-training qualifications but with relevant qualifications and experience. Participants generally have to complete a period of two years of in-service training as a licensed teacher before achieving qualified teacher status. The Government has also made it easier for teachers trained abroad to take up posts in English and Welsh schools. Trained teachers from other European Community countries are automatically granted qualified teacher status, while non-Community teachers undergo a training and evaluation period of between three months and two years.

Scotland

In Scotland all teachers in education authority schools must be registered with the General Teaching Council for Scotland. It is government policy that all entrants to the teaching profession should be graduates. New primary teachers qualify either through a four-year BEd course or a one-year postgraduate course of teacher training at a college of education. In addition, the University of Stirling offers courses which combine academic and professional training for those intending to become primary and secondary teachers. Teachers of academic subjects at secondary schools must hold a degree containing two passes in the subjects which they wish to teach. Secondary teachers must undertake a one-year postgraduate training course. For music and technology, four-year BEd courses are also available, and for physical education all teachers take BEd courses.

All courses have been revised following recommendations of working parties on teacher training. All new pre-service and major in-service courses provided by colleges of education must be approved by the Scottish Office Education Department and a validating body. Education authorities are to be asked to implement national guidelines for the introduction of systematic schemes of staff development and appraisal. The Government has taken reserve powers requiring authorities to operate schemes prescribed by it in the event of a breakdown of voluntary agreements.

Northern Ireland

Teacher training is provided by the two universities and two colleges of education. The principal courses are BEd Honours (four years), BA Honours (Education) and the one-year Post-graduate Certificate of Education. Education and library boards have the statutory duty to ensure that teachers are equipped with the necessary skills to implement education reforms and the Northern Ireland Curriculum.

Education-business Links

The Government considers that co-operation between the education system and business is essential to help people of all ages acquire the skills necessary to maintain Britain's position as a leading industrial and trading nation.

Much is being done under the Government's Technical and Vocational Education Initiative (TVEI—see p. 27), to which £900 million has been allotted from 1987 to 1997, and through Education Business Partnerships (see p. 52). As a result of these and other initiatives, matters relating to industry and commerce are being embedded in the curricula of schools, colleges and universities and in examinations. The relevance of classroom activities to working life was central to the thinking behind the introduction of the General Certificate of Secondary Education and the National Curriculum (see p. 27). In Scotland this led to the introduction of Standard Grade and revised Higher examinations (see p. 29) and other developments.

Businessmen and women are involved in curriculum development and enterprise activities for schoolchildren. In addition, they are represented in greater numbers on the governing bodies of schools and other institutions.

A shift in provision is occurring in post-school education from the arts and social sciences towards science, engineering, technology and directly vocational courses. Business and post-school education institutions are being encouraged to collaborate more closely for their mutual benefit. The latter may give enterprise training to students under the Government's Enterprise in Higher Education scheme to help students acquire the expertise required by industry.

Secondary School Education

Government policy is to ensure that every year 10 per cent of teachers should be given the opportunity to gain some business experience; and that every trainee teacher should have an appreciation of the needs of employers. Some 30,000 teachers spent time working in industry during 1991–92 under a scheme administered by the Confederation of British Industry.

The Government also wants all pupils to have at least two weeks' work experience before leaving school. More than 71 per cent of schoolchildren aged 15–16 undertook work experience placements in 1989. In addition, increasing numbers are undertaking vocational work experience and work-shadowing placements between the ages of 16 and 18. City technology colleges, sponsored by industry and commerce, provide a broadly based secondary education for girls and boys of all abilities.

Under the Compacts scheme launched by the Government in 1988, there are local agreements between employers, local education authorities and training providers. Young people, supported by their school or college, work to reach agreed targets, and employers undertake to provide a job with training, or training leading to a job, for those attaining the targets. Some 700 schools are participating in Compact schemes and 140,000 young people are involved. The Government is making available more than £28 million over four years from 1990 to support Compacts, which are being extended nationwide. The Belfast Compact scheme aims to guarantee an interview for a job to students who meet their personal targets.

Local Education Business Partnerships are formal bodies of senior representatives from education, business and the wider community. Members work together to co-ordinate school and college education/business links and develop activities in their local areas. Government funds for partnerships (£5 million in the period between 1991 and 1993) are distributed through Training and Enterprise Councils.

Post-school Education

A network of 82 employer-led Training and Enterprise Councils (TECs) in England and Wales is intended to make training and enterprise activities more relevant to the needs of employers and individuals locally. In Scotland, 22 Local Enterprise Companies (LECs) have a similar role. The Training and Employment Agency is responsible for training and employment programmes and activities in Northern Ireland.

Some TECs and LECs, working in close co-operation with LEAs and other education interests, have been running pilot schemes of Training Credits, which offer an entitlement to train to approved standards for young people leaving full-time education.

Over 40 science parks have been set up by higher education institutions in conjunction with industrial scientists and technologists to promote the development and commercial application of advanced technology. There are plans to establish more science parks. In addition, the Government has set up a network of regional technology centres to promote technology transfer and related training services. The centres are collaborative ventures involving colleges and universities working with local firms and a number are now operating on a commercial basis, their income being earned from the services provided.

The Government's LINK scheme aims to encourage firms to work jointly with higher education institutions on government-funded research relevant to industrial needs.

Adult Education

Adult education is provided in further education colleges, adult colleges and centres and by voluntary bodies. In April 1993 the duty to provide adult education will be divided between new further education funding councils and LEAs. The former will be responsible for courses leading to academic and vocational qualifications, basic skills courses, English as a second language courses, and courses on communications skills for students with learning difficulties. LEAs will be responsible for securing other types of further education for adults.

In addition to cultural and craft pursuits, students may follow courses leading to academic and vocational qualifications, and courses which provide access to higher education.

ALBSU

The Adult Literacy and Basic Skills Unit (ALBSU) is concerned with adult literacy, numeracy and communications skills in England and Wales. It provides consultancy and advisory services, funds local development projects, produces and publishes materials for teachers and students and sponsors staff training. Government grant to ALBSU totals £3.2 million in 1992–93.

In January 1991 the Government announced a new £3 million programme, Basic Skills at Work, on literacy and numeracy skills for adults. It is designed to encourage LEAs and TECs to work together to improve the provision of basic skills. It is targeted at unemployed people and those in work who cannot progress without improved basic skills.

In Scotland, responsibility for overseeing adult basic education rests with the Scottish Community Education Council.

Open College

Open learning opportunities have been extended with the formation in 1987 of the Open College, an independent company set up with government support. The College brings together broadcasters, educationists and sponsors, and provides vocational education and training courses below degree level. Up to £12 million is being allocated by the Government for the College's commercial activities as well as £6 million for broadcasting. Programmes are broadcast by Channel 4 television. The Open College of the Arts, also launched in 1987, offers an art foundation course to those wishing to study at home.

National Institute of Adult Continuing Education

The National Institute of Adult Continuing Education is a centre of information, research, development work and publication for adult and continuing education. Its functions are to:

—advise and co-ordinate policy and practice; and

—act as a channel of communication for the organisations it represents.

Scottish Community Education Council

The Scottish Community Education Council advises the Government and promotes all community education matters, including adult literacy and basic education, and the youth service in Scotland.

Educational Links Overseas

Large numbers of people come to Britain from overseas to study, and British people work and train overseas. The British aid programme encourages links between educational institutions in Britain and developing countries.

British membership of the European Community has created closer ties with the other member countries. In schools, colleges and universities in Britain there has been an expansion of interest in European studies and languages, with exchanges of teachers, schoolchildren and students taking place.

The exchange of students is promoted by the Community's European Action Scheme for Mobility of University Students (ERASMUS) under which grants are provided to enable Community students to study in other member states. Some 19,000 students from Britain have benefited from the scheme.

The Community's LINGUA programme seeks to encourage the teaching and learning of foreign languages throughout the Community. It gives grants towards joint educational projects and exchanges for young people undergoing professional, vocational and technical education; it also covers measures to develop language training materials for business.

The European Community Action Programme for Education and Training for Technology (COMETT) aims to foster co-operation between higher education establishments and commercial enterprises in technological training.

Community member states have created nine European schools, including one at Culham, Oxfordshire, to provide a multinational education for the children of staff employed in Community institutions.

Overseas Students in Britain

People come to Britain from all over the world to study. British universities and other further and higher education establishments have built up their reputation overseas by offering tuition of the highest standards, maintaining low student-to-staff ratios, and offering relevant courses and qualifications.

In the academic year 1990–91 there were about 87,000 overseas students at universities and other public sector establishments of further and higher education. In addition, many thousands of people from abroad were training for nursing, law, banking and accountancy, and service and other industries. About 40 per cent of all overseas students were from the Commonwealth and Britain's dependent territories. There were about 26,000 from the other European Community member states.

About a third of students enrolled for full-time postgraduate study or research in Britain in 1990–91 came from overseas. Several British colleges of further education have entered into arrangements with British universities to provide bridging courses for overseas students before they enter university.

Most overseas students pay their own fees and expenses or hold awards from their own governments. Those following courses of higher or further education pay fees which cover the full cost of their courses. Nationals of other member countries of the European Community generally pay the lower level of fees that applies to British students; where their courses are designated for mandatory awards they may be eligible for fees-only awards from LEAs.

Government Scholarship Schemes

The Government makes considerable provision for students and trainees from overseas under its overseas aid programme and other award and scholarship schemes. In 1990–91 nearly 25,000 overseas students were supported, including some studying overseas, at a cost of more than £140 million. The majority were from developing countries, mainly in the Commonwealth, studying under the Technical Co-operation and Training Programme, which is financed from the aid programme.

Under the Overseas Development Administration Shared Scholarship Scheme, 190 awards were offered in 1991–92, primarily at postgraduate level, for students from the developing countries of the Commonwealth, with costs being shared between the British Government and the educational institutions.

The Foreign & Commonwealth Office Scholarships and Awards Scheme (FCOSAS), which operates in some 140 countries, is designed to bring to Britain present and future leaders, decision-makers and formers of opinion. A notable feature of the FCOSAS is the increasing number of awards jointly financed by the Foreign & Commonwealth Office in partnership with the private sector and academic institutions. The Department of Trade and Industry also finances a trade-related scholarship scheme in partnership with British industry.

Outside the aid programme, the Overseas Research Students Awards Scheme, funded by the Department for Education, provides assistance for overseas research students of high ability to attend British universities.

Other Schemes

Many public and private scholarships and fellowships are available to students from overseas and to British students who want to study overseas. Among the best known, and open to men and women in all walks of life, are the British Council Scholarships, the Commonwealth Scholarship and Fellowship Plan, the Fulbright Scholarship Scheme, the Marshall Scholarships, the Rhodes Scholarships, the Churchill Scholarships and the Confederation of British Industry Scholarships. Most British universities and colleges offer scholarships for which graduates of any nationality are eligible.

English as a Foreign Language

The continuing increase in interest in English as a foreign language is reflected in the growth of public sector English language courses and in the number of private language schools in Britain. Over 240 private schools are recognised by the British Council. The Council has English language teaching centres in other countries and also runs a programme for teaching English related to specific jobs and skills. Other British language schools have offices overseas, enabling people to learn English in their own countries, while in Britain university language and linguistics departments are an important resource. The Government's aid programme supports the teaching of English in many developing countries by financing major projects in schools, universities and other institutions. Publications and other material relating to English language teaching have increased in number and are now a large component in many publishers' lists, constituting a major export.

BBC English, the English-teaching arm of the BBC's World Service, offers a worldwide facility for the individual learner at home on radio and, with the advent of the new World Service Television operation, increasingly on television.

Educational Exchanges

British Council
The British Council promotes cultural and educational relations with other countries. It plays an important part in the management of the aid programme to education. Its main functions are to:

—recruit teachers for work overseas;

—organise short overseas visits by British experts;

—encourage cultural exchange visits; and

—foster academic interchange between British higher education institutions and those in other countries.

Co-operation between higher education in Britain and developing countries is promoted with funding from the Overseas Development Administration. It is brought about through recruiting staff for overseas universities, the secondment of staff from British higher education establishments, interdepartmental faculty links, local staff development, short-term teaching and advisory visits, and general consultancy services.

Central Bureau for Educational Visits and Exchanges
Funded by the Government, the national Central Bureau for Educational Visits and Exchanges provides information and advice on all forms of educational visits and exchanges. It also:

—administers and develops a wide range of curriculum-related exchange schemes;

—links educational establishments and local education authorities with their counterparts in other countries; and

—organises meetings, workshops and conferences on professional international experience.

The Bureau administers teacher exchanges in Europe and the United States, short courses for language teachers and international study visits. Opportunities for young people include school and class links and English language summer camps. For the post-16 age group, there are work placements and English language assistants' posts, as well as other exchange programmes.

Association of Commonwealth Universities

The Association of Commonwealth Universities promotes contact and co-operation between nearly 400 member universities in 31 Commonwealth countries or regions. It assists student and staff mobility by administering award schemes, including, for Britain, the Commonwealth Scholarship and Fellowship Plan and the Overseas Development Administration Shared Scholarship Scheme, and by operating an academic appointments service. It publishes information about Commonwealth universities, courses and scholarships, and organises meetings in different parts of the world.

Other Organisations

The Commonwealth Education Liaison Committee supplements normal direct dealings on education between Commonwealth countries. The United Kingdom Council for Overseas Student Affairs is an independent body serving overseas students, and those concerned with student affairs.

The Youth Exchange Centre, managed by the British Council, gives advice, information, training and grants to British youth groups involved in international exchanges. The Centre is the national agency for the European Community-sponsored exchange scheme, Youth for Europe.

The Youth Service

The purpose of the youth service is to provide young people with opportunities to help them develop their potential as individuals in the transition from childhood to adult life. It is a diverse service managed by local authorities and voluntary bodies. In England the National Youth Agency, which is funded by the Government, promotes the partnership between local authorities and voluntary bodies and supports both elements of the service. It is also involved in youth worker training, support for managers of organisations within the service and support for international work. It also collects and publishes information on youth service matters.

The Welsh Office provides grant aid to national youth service bodies with headquarters in Wales and has established a Wales Youth Agency, which is similar to the Agency in England.

In Scotland the youth service forms a part of adult education, which is integrated within community education. The Scottish Community Education Council has the role of promoting community education. The Youth Council for Northern Ireland, with executive and advisory powers, was set up in 1990.

Voluntary Youth Organisations

National voluntary youth organisations undertake the major share of youth activities through local groups which raise most of their day-to-day expenses by their own efforts. Many receive financial and other help from LEAs, which also make available facilities in many areas. The wide variety of organisations include the uniformed Scouts and Girl Guides, church-based groups and organisations for Jews and Muslims. Others are concerned with sport, the arts and the environment. Many local authorities and voluntary youth organisations have responded to new needs in society by making provision, for example, for the young unemployed, young people from the ethnic minorities, young people in inner cities or rural areas and those in trouble or especially vulnerable. Other areas of concern are homelessness and provision for handicapped young people.

Many authorities have youth committees on which official and voluntary bodies are represented, and employ youth officers to co-ordinate youth work and to arrange in-service training. There are also youth councils, which are representative bodies of young people from local youth organisations.

The Duke of Edinburgh's Award Scheme operates through local authorities, schools, youth organisations and industrial firms. It enables young people from Britain and other Commonwealth countries to take part, with voluntary help from adults, in a variety of challenging activities in four areas: community service, expeditions, the development of personal interests and social and practical skills, and physical recreation.

Youth Workers

In England and Wales a two-year training course at certain universities and higher education colleges leads to the status of qualified youth and community worker; several undergraduate part-time courses and postgraduate courses are also available. In Scotland one-, two- and three-year courses are provided at colleges of education and in Northern Ireland courses are run by the University of Ulster.

An estimated 6,000 full-time youth workers are supported by some 535,000 part-time workers, both qualified and unqualified, many of them unpaid. Short courses and conferences are held on youth and community work. There are also in-service courses for serving youth workers and officers. Initial and in-service courses are professionally validated by the National Youth Agency. Youth counselling is supported by the National Association of Young People's Counselling and Advisory Services.

Voluntary Service by Young People

Thousands of young people voluntarily undertake community service designed to help those in need, including elderly and disabled people, and many others work on environmental projects. Organisations providing opportunities for community service, such as Community Service Volunteers, International Voluntary Service and the British Trust for Conservation Volunteers, receive grants from the Government. Many schools also organise community service work as part of the curriculum, and voluntary work in the community is sponsored by a number of churches.

Young Volunteers in the Community is a national scheme which recruits young people aged 16 to 24 to work on a variety of community projects for 12 to 18 weeks.

Addresses

Government Departments

Department for Education, Sanctuary Buildings, Great Smith Street, London SW1P 3BT.

Department of Education for Northern Ireland, Rathgael House, Balloo Road, Bangor, County Down BT19 7PR.

Department of Employment, Caxton House, Tothill Street, London SW1H 9NF.

Foreign and Commonwealth Office, King Charles Street, London SW1A 2AH.

Office for Standards in Education, Elizabeth House, York Road, London SE1 7PH.

Scottish Office Education Department, New St Andrew's House, Edinburgh EH1 3SY.

Welsh Office Education Department, Government Buildings, Ty-Glas Road, Llanishen, Cardiff CF4 5WE.

Other Organisations

The British Council, 10 Spring Gardens, London SW1A 2BN.

Adult Literacy and Basic Skills Unit, 229 High Holborn, London WC1V 7DA.

City and Guilds of London Institute, 46 Britannia Street, London WC1X 9RG.

Duke of Edinburgh's Award Scheme, 5 Prince of Wales Terrace, London W8 5PG.

General Teaching Council for Scotland, 5 Royal Terrace, Edinburgh EH7 5AF.

National Institute of Adult and Continuing Education, 19b De Montfort Street, Leicester LE1 7GE.

National Foundation for Educational Research in England and Wales, The Mere, Upton Park, Slough, Berkshire SL1 2DQ.

The Open College, 101 Wigmore Street, London W1H 0AX.

The Open University, Walton Hall, Milton Keynes MK7 6AA.

Scottish Council for Research in Education, 15 St John Street, Edinburgh EH8 8JR.

Scottish Community Education Council, West Coates House, 90 Haymarket Terrace, Edinburgh EH12 6LQ.

Scottish Consultative Council on the Curriculum, 17 St John Street, Edinburgh EH8 8DG.

Scottish Vocational Education Council, Hanover House, 24 Douglas Street, Glasgow G2 7NQ.

National Council for Vocational Qualifications, 222 Euston Road, London NW1 2BZ.

National Curriculum Council, 15/17 New Street, York YO1 2RA.

National Council for Educational Technology, 3 Devonshire Street, London W1N 2BA.

School Examinations and Assessment Council, Newcombe House, 45 Notting Hill Gate, London W11 3JB.

Scottish Examination Board, 15 Ironmills Road, Dalkeith, Edinburgh EH22 1LE.

Further Reading

			£
Access and Opportunity: A Strategy for Education and Training. Cm 1530. ISBN 0 10 115302 3	HMSO	1991	5.50
Choice and Diversity: A New Framework for Schools. Cm 2021. ISBN 0 10 120212 1.	HMSO	1991	8.60
Education and Training for the 21st Century Cm 1536 (two volumes). ISBN 0 10 115362 7.	HMSO	1991	11.00
Higher Education: A New Framework. Cm 1541. ISBN 0 10 115412 7.	HMSO	1991	6.60

Acronyms and Abbreviations

ALBSU	Adult Literacy and Basic Skills Unit
BTEC	Business and Technology Education Council
CATE	Council for the Accreditation of Teacher Education
CNAA	Council for National Academic Awards
COMETT	European Community Action Programme for Education and Training for Technology
ERASMUS	European Community Action Scheme for the Mobility of University Students
FCOSAS	Foreign & Commonwealth Office Scholarships and Awards Scheme
GCE	General Certificate of Education
GCSE	General Certificate of Secondary Education
LEAs	Local education authorities
LECs	Local Enterprise Companies
NCET	National Council for Educational Technology
NCVQ	National Council for Vocational Qualifications
OFSTED	Office for Standards in Education
PCAS	Polytechnics Central Admissions System
PGCE	Postgraduate Certificate of Education
SCE	Scottish Certificate of Education
SCOTVEC	Scottish Vocational Education Council
TECs	Training and Enterprise Councils
TVEI	Technical and Vocational Education Initiative
UCCA	Universities Central Council for Admissions

Index

Printed in the UK for HMSO.
Dd 0295906, 12/92, C30, 51-2432, 5673.

A MONTHLY UPDATE

CURRENT AFFAIRS:
A MONTHLY SURVEY

Using the latest authoritative information from official and other sources, *Current Affairs* is an invaluable digest of important developments in all areas of British affairs. Focusing on policy initiatives and other topical issues, its factual approach makes it the ideal companion for *Britain Handbook* and *Aspects of Britain*. Separate sections deal with governmental; international; economic; and social, cultural and environmental affairs. A further section provides details of recent documentary sources for these areas. There is also a twice-yearly index.

Annual subscription including index and postage £35·80 net.
Binder £4·95.

Buyers of Britain 1993: An Official Handbook *qualify for a discount of 25 per cent on a year's subscription to* Current Affairs *(see next page)*.

HMSO Publications Centre
(Mail and telephone orders only)
PO Box 276
LONDON SW8 5DT
Telephone orders: 071 873 9090

THE ANNUAL PICTURE

BRITAIN
1993

AN OFFICIAL HANDBOOK

BRITAIN HANDBOOK

The annual picture of Britain is provided by *Britain: An Official Handbook* - the forty-fourth edition will be published early in 1993. It is the unrivalled reference book about Britain, packed with information and statistics on every facet of British life.

With a circulation of over 20,000 worldwide, it is essential for libraries, educational institutions, business organisations and individuals needing easy access to reliable and up-to-date information, and is supported in this role by its sister publication, *Current Affairs: A Monthly Survey*.

Approx. 500 pages; 24 pages of colour illustrations; 16 maps; diagrams and tables throughout the text; and a statistical section. Price £19·50.

Buyers of Britain 1993: An Official Handbook *have the opportunity of a year's subscription to* Current Affairs *at 25 per cent off the published price of £35·80. They will also have the option of renewing their subscription next year at the same discount. Details in each copy of* Handbook, *from HMSO Publications Centre and at HMSO bookshops (see back of title page).*